The Wisdom of Cats

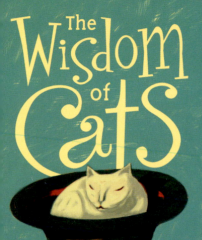

Illustrations by **Beppe Giacobbe**

Lawrence Teacher Books
— Philadelphia —

Mechanicals produced by book soup publishing, inc.
Cover and interior design by Susan Van Horn
Illustrations © 2000 by Beppe Giacobbe
Quotes compiled by Corey Schmidt
Edited by Erin Slonaker

ISBN 1-930408-07-2

10 9 8 7 6 5 4 3 2 1

Please support your local book or gift store. However,
if you cannot find this book there, you may order it
directly from the publisher. Please add $1.50 for postage
and handling. Send check or money order to
the address below.

Lawrence Teacher Books
2611 Bainbridge Street
Philadelphia, PA 19146

Contents

Introduction ~ ~ ~ ~ ~ ~ ~ ~ ~ ~ ~ 4

In Their Own Words ✱ ✱ ✱ ✱ ✱ ✱ ✱ ✱ 9

Cats and Their Owners — . — . — 28

What It Is to Be a Cat ✱ ✱ ✱ ✱ ✱ ✱ ✱ 54

Lessons to Be Learned ~ ~ ~ ~ ~ 92

Introduction

*There is, indeed, no single quality
of the cat that man could not emulate
to his advantage.*

~ ~ ~ ~ ~ ~ ~ ~ ~ ~

—Carl Van Vechten (1880–1964)

Independent, resourceful, honest, mystical, loyal, clever—with qualities like these, who wouldn't want to be more like the cat? As the subject of countless stories, poems, and books, the cat is always the cunning survivor who triumphs over its adversaries. Cared for but never owned, mankind's feline fascination traces back more than 4,000 years, when cats were worshipped as gods. Observing cats has since become a national pastime. They are the beloved stars of classic fairy tales, popular novels, and syndicated comic strips. But their best role is performed in our very own living rooms in front of their best audience, their caretakers.

The cat has captured the attention of everyone from poets to politicians, historians to humorists, artists to aristocrats.

So what is it about the cat that makes it the subject of such awe and admiration? Serving as a metaphor for mankind, its idiosyncrasies, strengths, needs, and complexities mirror our own. Defining the enigma of the cat undermines her very uniqueness. But that certainly hasn't stopped anyone from trying. The cat has captivated behavioral scientists, who have written litanies to their true and deepest natures. Quite simply, their companionship elevates our ordinary lives.

Humanity would be greatly transformed if we could learn the lessons of the feline, if we could adopt just some of their attributes, or benefit from the knowledge acquired in just one of their nine lives. Exploring our symbiotic connection to these compatible creatures causes us to reflect on our own foibles and follies. We celebrate the cat by examining its nine lives—lives lived with loyalty and instinct, independence, mystery, tranquility, cleverness, communication, conceit, and persistence. Perhaps by reading these quotes of worldly wisdom, we can improve our own lives and come just one step closer to being more like the cat.

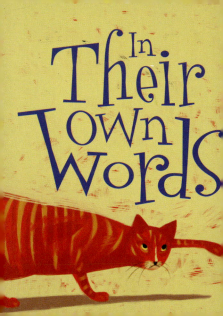

In Their Own Words

Relationships are difficult, particularly between two individuals of different species.

✳ ✳ ✳ ✳ ✳ ✳ ✳ ✳ ✳ ✳ ✳

Bomber the Cat, in *Conversations with My Cat*, by David Fisher, American writer (b. 1946)

Sleeping is underrated. So is

stretching.

Suzy Becker, American writer
(b. 1962), in *All I Need to Know
I Learned From My Cat*

There's a good reason cats say

rather than

We-ow or you-ow.

Bomber the Cat, in *Conversations with My Cat,* by David Fisher, American writer (b. 1946)

To know me
is to love me.

~~~~~~~~~~~

Morris the Cat, 9 Lives spokescat

Never trifle with the

affections

of a woman!

– · – · – · – · – · –

Catwoman, *Batman,* the animated series

The sound of a can opener is the only thing that makes me feel truly alive.

* * * * * * * * * * *

Salem the Cat, *Sabrina the Teenage Witch,* television show

15

Make your
own hours.

~~~~~~~~~~~~

Suzy Becker, American writer
(b. 1962), in *All I Need to Know
I Learned From My Cat*

I think it's fine
To be feline
It's very nice
If you are not mice.

— · — · — · — · — ·

Fluffy Yeats, 20th century
Feline-American poet

The golden rule of cats

that governs all relationships

we have with people:

you scratch my back,

you scratch my back.

* * * * * * * * * *

Bomber the Cat, in *Conversations with My Cat,* by David Fisher, American writer (b. 1946)

Don't be afraid to take chances. Somehow, you'll always land on your feet.

~ ~ ~ ~ ~ ~ ~ ~ ~ ~ ~

Suzy Becker, American writer (b. 1962), in *All I Need to Know I Learned From My Cat*

If you don't

indulge

yourself, nobody will.

Garfield, American comic strip
character, by Jim Davis, American
cartoonist (b. 1945)

Well then, a dog growls when it's angry and wags its tail when it's pleased. Now, I growl when I'm pleased and wag my tail when I'm angry. Therefore I'm *mad*.

Cheshire Cat, in *Alice's Adventures in Wonderland,* by Lewis Carroll, British writer (1832—1898)

Humans will always
be lucky if they know
how to make friends
with strange cats.

~ ~ ~ ~ ~ ~ ~ ~ ~ ~ ~

Colonial American cat proverb

People make great companions
for cats because they practically
take care of themselves . . .
all a cat has to do is

purr and rub

against their legs every now and
then and then they're content.

* * * * * * * * * * *

Morris the Cat, 9 Lives spokescat

Cats are *poetry* in motion.

Dogs are gibberish in neutral.

— . — . — . — . — . —

**Garfield, American comic strip
character, by Jim Davis, American
cartoonist (b. 1945)**

People think;
cats feel.

~ ~ ~ ~ ~ ~ ~ ~ ~ ~ ~

Bomber the Cat, in *Conversations
with My Cat,* by David Fisher,
American writer (b. 1946)

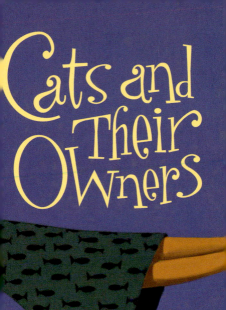

In the matter of animals I love
only cats, but I love them

unreasonably,

for their qualities and in spite
of their numerous faults.

* * * * * * * * * * *

J. K. Huysmans,
French novelist (1848 –1907)

There are few things in life
more heartwarming than to
be welcomed by a cat.

— · — · — · — · — · —

Tay Hohoff, American writer,
editor (1898—1974)

When I play with my cat who knows whether I do not make her more Sport than she makes me?

~ ~ ~ ~ ~ ~ ~ ~ ~ ~

Michel de Montaigne,
French essayist (1533–1592)

"I'm letting her know that I don't need her to come to me, that it's not desperate or urgent or anything . . . just that this is where the love and the petting are."

No sooner had he explained than the cat appeared on the top of his hip, purring, nuzzling, and demanding his attention. "And that, my dear, is the right way to lure a cat."

* * * * * * * * * * *

L. F. Hoffman, American writer (b. 1944), in *The Bachelor's Cat*

I got rid of my husband.

The cat was allergic.

— · — · — · — · — · —

Anonymous

What greater gift
than the love of a cat?

~ ~ ~ ~ ~ ~ ~ ~ ~ ~ ~

Charles Dickens,
British writer (1812–1870)

To gain the friendship of a cat is a difficult thing. The cat is a philosophical, methodical, quiet animal, tenacious of its own habits, fond of order and cleanliness, and it does not lightly confer its friendship. If you are worthy of its affection, a cat will be your friend, but never your slave. He keeps his free will, though he loves, and he will not do for you what he thinks is unreasonable. But if he once gives himself to you it is with absolute confidence and affection.

* * * * * * * * * * *

Theophile Gautier, French poet (1811—1872)

Garfield's Law:

Cats instinctively know
the precise moment their owners
will awaken . . . then they awaken
them ten minutes sooner.

— . — . — . — . — . —

Jim Davis, American cartoonist (b. 1945)

The really great thing about cats is their endless variety. One can pick a cat to fit almost any kind of décor, color scheme, income, personality, mood. But under the fur, whatever color it may be, there still lies, essentially unchanged, one of the world's free souls.

~ ~ ~ ~ ~ ~ ~ ~ ~

Eric Gurney, 20th century American cartoonist, writer

The wildcat is the "real" cat,
the soul of the domestic cat;
unknowable to human beings,
he yet exists inside our house-
hold pets, who have long ago
seduced us with their
seemingly civilized ways.

* * * * * * * * * *

Joyce Carol Oates,
American writer (b. 1938)

40

*Happy is the home
with at least one cat.*

— · — · — · — · — · — ·

Italian proverb

To **understand** a cat, you must realize that he has his own gifts, his own viewpoint, even his own morality.

~~~~~~~~~~~~~~

**Lillian Jackson Braun,
American writer (b. 1916)**

42

As every cat owner knows,
nobody owns a cat.

* * * * * * * * * * *

Ellen Perry Berkeley, American writer,
cat observationist (b. 1931)

The cat is domestic only as far as suits its own ends. . . .

— · — · — · — · —

Saki (H. H. Munro), British writer
(1870—1916), in *The Achievement of the Cat*

It's really the cat's house.

I just pay the mortgage.

~ ~ ~ ~ ~ ~ ~ ~ ~ ~ ~

Anonymous

Cats are mysterious
beings. . . . You never know
if they love you or if they

condescend

to occupy your house.

* * * * * * * * * * *

Paul Moore, American clergyman,
writer (1917–1976)

It's all in the feline choreography of living and loving: the quietest room, the softest pillow, when and where the sun's rays are kindest, who keeps the tidbits, and which trees offer the most frolic and the fastest escape. The perfect earthly dancer—the cat.

— . — . — . — . —

Julie Newmar, TV's Catwoman (b. 1935)

There's no need for a piece of sculpture in a home that has a cat.

~ ~ ~ ~ ~ ~ ~ ~ ~ ~ ~

William Bates, American writer
(1860—1931)

I love cats because I enjoy my home; and little by little, they become its visible Soul.

* * * * * * * * * * *

Jean Cocteau, French writer,
director, poet (1889–1963)

The difference between a cat and a dog: A dog thinks, "They feed me, they shelter me, they love me, they must be gods." A cat thinks, "They feed me, they shelter me, they love me, I must be God."

— . — . — . — . — .

Anonymous

A home without a cat, and
a well-fed, well-petted, and
properly revered cat, may be
a perfect home, perhaps, but
how can it prove its title?

~ ~ ~ ~ ~ ~ ~ ~ ~ ~

Mark Twain, American writer (1835–1910)

Cats always know whether people like or dislike them. They do not always *care* enough to do anything about it.

* * * * * * * * * * *

Winifred Carrière, 20th century American writer

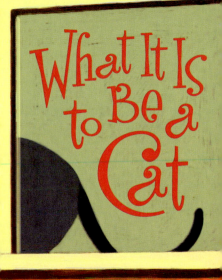

Cats love subtly, with nuances that could easily be missed. . . . The way she loves is quiet and gentle, and if a love like that ever crept into my heart on two legs as softly as those little cat feet, I'd be purring for the rest of my life.

— · — · · — · · — · — · —

Beth Fowler, American writer (b. 1940), in *Could You Love Me Like My Cat?*

Cat: a pygmy lion who loves mice, hates dogs, and patronizes *human beings.*

~~~~~~~~~~

Oliver Herford, American writer, illustrator (1863–1936)

Cats don't bark and act brave when they see something small in fur or feathers, they kill it. Dogs tend to bravado. They're braggarts. In the great evolutionary drama, the dog is Sergeant Bilko, the cat is Rambo.

* * * * * * * * * *

James Gorman, American journalist, writer (b. 1949)

A cat has

absolute honesty.

Ernest Hemingway,
American writer (1899—1961)

The cat, it is well to remember, remains the friend of man because it **pleases him** to do so and not because he must.

Carl Van Vechten,
American photographer (1880–1964)

~~~~~~~~~~

Dogs come when they're called;
cats take a message
and get back to you later.

* * * * * * * * * * *

Mary Bly, American writer (b. 1948)

Of all God's creatures there is only one that cannot be made the slave of the lash. That one is the cat. If man could be crossed with the cat it would improve man, but it would deteriorate *the cat.*

—.—.—.—.—.—

Mark Twain, American writer (1835–1910)

Are cats lazy? Well, more power to them if they are. Which one of us has not

entertained

the dream of doing just as he likes, when and how he likes, and as much as he likes?

~ ~ ~ ~ ~ ~ ~

Fernand Mery, French writer, animal behaviorist, veterinarian (1897 – 1984)

The cat is the individualist,
the aberrant; he is the creature
who has never run in packs nor
fought in herds nor thought in
congregations. He has the dignity
of the self-contained and the
confidence of the self-sufficient.

✳ ✳ ✳ ✳ ✳ ✳ ✳ ✳ ✳ ✳

Francis Lockridge (1896–1963) and Richard
Lockridge (1898-1982), American writers,
in *Cats and People*

I wish I could write as

mysterious

as a cat.

—··—··—··—··—··—

Edgar Allan Poe,
American poet, writer (1809–1849)

The cat is cryptic
and close to strange things
which men cannot see.

~ ~ ~ ~ ~ ~ ~ ~ ~ ~ ~

H. P. Lovecraft,
American writer (1890–1937)

Cats are mysterious kind of folk—
there is more passing in their
minds than we are aware of.

Sir Walter Scott, Scottish poet, writer,
historian (1771–1832)

A computer and a cat are somewhat alike—they both purr, and like to be stroked, and spend a lot of the day

motionless.

They also have secrets they don't necessarily share.

— . — . — . — . —

John Updike, American writer (b. 1932)

It is in their eyes that their
magic resides.

~ ~ ~ ~ ~ ~ ~ ~

Arthur Symons, British poet
(1865–1945)

To reSpect *the*
cat is the beginning
of the aesthetic sense.

* * * * * * * * * * *

Erasmus Darwin,
British physician, poet (1731–1802)

The cat is, above all, a
dramatist.

— . — . — . — . — . — . —

Margaret Benson,
20th century American writer

73

If animals could speak, the
dog would be a blundering,
outspoken, honest fellow—
but the cat would have the
rare grace of never saying
a word too much.

~ ~ ~ ~ ~ ~ ~ ~ ~ ~

Philip Gilbert Hamerton,
British artist, essayist (1834–1894)

*A little drowsing cat is
an image of perfect*

beatitude.

* * * * * * * * * * * *

Champfleury, French writer (1821—1889)

Like a graceful vase,
a cat even when motionless
seems to flow.

— · — · · — · · — · · — · —

George F. Will, American political commentator (b. 1941)

Dogs eat.

Cats dine.

~ ~ ~ ~ ~ ~ ~ ~ ~ ~ ~

Ann Taylor, British poet (1782—1866)

Cats are *smarter* than dogs. You can't get eight cats to pull a sled through snow.

* * * * * * * * * * *

Jeff Valdez, 20th century
American comedian

The cat seldom interferes with other people's rights. His

intelligence

keeps him from doing many of the things that complicate life.

Carl Van Vechten,
American photographer (1880—1964)

A cat is an example of

Sophistication

minus civilization.

~ ~ ~ ~ ~ ~ ~ ~ ~ ~

Anonymous

A cat can be trusted to purr
when she is pleased,
which is more than can be said
for human beings.

* * * * * * * * * * *

William Ralph Inge,
Anglican prelate, writer (1860–1954)

It is a very inconvenient
habit of kittens (Alice had
once made the remark) that,
whatever you say to them,
they always purr.

— . — . — . — . —

Lewis Carroll,
British writer (1832—1898)

Cats have a contempt of speech. Why should they talk when they can communicate without words?

~~~~~~~~~

Lillian Jackson Braun,
American writer (b. 1916)

Thousands of years ago, cats
were **Worshipped** as gods.
Cats have never forgotten this.

* * * * * * * * * *

Anonymous

Nothing's more
determined
than a cat on a hot tin roof. . . .

— . — . — . — . —

Tennessee Williams,
American playwright (1911–1983)

With the qualities of cleanliness, discretion, affection, patience, dignity, and courage that cats have, how many of us, I ask you, would be capable of being cats?

Fernand Mery, French writer,
animal behaviorist,
veterinarian (1897–1984)

I am as

Vigilant

as a cat to

steal cream.

* * * * * * * * * * *

William Shakespeare,
English playwright, poet (1564–1616)

Cats don't like change
without their consent.

— • — • — • — • —

Roger A. Caras, American animal
photographer, writer, wildlife
preservationist (b. 1928)

A dog, I have always said, is prose; a cat is a poem.

Jean Burden, American writer (b. 1914)

Lessons to Be Learned

Men and dogs will

never understand

what a woman sees in a cat.

* * * * * * * * * * *

Anonymous

Even overweight cats
instinctively know the
cardinal rule: when fat,
arrange yourself in

Slim poses.

— · — · — · — · — · —

John Weitz, American clothes
designer (b. 1922)

Way down deep, we're
all motivated by the

Same urges.

Cats have the courage
to live by them.

~ ~ ~ ~ ~ ~ ~ ~ ~ ~

Jim Davis, American cartoonist (b. 1945)

There are two means of refuge from the miseries of life: music and cats.

* * * * * * * * * *

Albert Schweitzer, German doctor, humanitarian, philosopher (1875–1965)

If you want to know the

character

of a man, find out what his

cat thinks of him.

— . — . — . — . — . —

Anonymous

Cats know how to obtain food without labor, shelter without confinement, and love without penalties.

~ ~ ~ ~ ~ ~ ~ ~ ~ ~ ~

W. L. George, American writer (1882–1926)

I've never understood why women love cats. Cats are independent, they don't listen, they don't come in when you call, they like to stay out all night, and when they're home they like to be left alone and sleep. In other words, every quality that women hate in a man, they love in a cat.

* * * * * * * * * *

Jay Leno, American talk-show host, comedian (b. 1950)

What sort of philosophers
are we who know absolutely

nothing

of the origin and destiny of cats?

— · — · — · — · — · —

Henry David Thoreau,
American philosopher (1817—1862)

We cannot, without

becoming cats,

perfectly understand

the mind of a cat.

~ ~ ~ ~ ~ ~ ~ ~ ~ ~

St. George Mivart,
British biologist (1827—1900)

Every cat is really the most

beautiful

woman in the room.

* * * * * * * * * * *

E. V. Lucas, British writer, essayist

(1868—1938)

In the middle of a world that had always been a bit mad, the cat walks with

~ ~ ~ ~ ~ ~ ~ ~ ~ ~ ~

Rosanne Amberson, 20th Century American writer

106

Even the stupidest cat
seems to know more
than any dog.

~~~~~~~~~~

**Eleanor Clark,
American writer (1913–1996)**

Cats seem to go on the principle that it *never* does any harm to ask for what you want.

* * * * * * * * * * *

Joseph Wood Krutch, American literary naturalist (1893—1970)

Meow is like aloha—
it can mean anything.

Hank Ketchum, American cartoonist,
creator of *Dennis the Menace* (b. 1920)

Never underestimate the

poWer

of a purr.

~ ~ ~ ~ ~ ~ ~ ~ ~ ~ ~

Anonymous

In a cat's eye all things belong to cats.

* * * * * * * * * * *

British saying

Purring

would seem to be, in her case,
an automatic safety-valve
device for dealing with
happiness overflow.

— · — · — · — · —

Monica Edwards, British writer (1912–1998)

All cats are possessed of a

proud Spirit

and the surest way to forfeit the

esteem of a cat is to treat him

as an inferior being.

~~~~~~~~~~

Michael Joseph, British writer (1914–1981)

If we are to take the cat at all, we must take him as he is, not as we are. He will meet us, but perhaps not quite half-way.

* * * * * * * * * * *

Francis Lockridge (1896–1963) and Richard Lockridge (1898–1982), American writers, in *Cats and People*

Any conditioned cat-hater
can be won over by any cat who
chooses to make the effort.

— · — · — · — · —

Paul Corey, American writer (b. 1903),
in *Do Cats Think?*

Cats are always elegant.

~~~~~~~~~~

John Weitz, American clothes
designer (b. 1922)

Cats find malicious

amusement

in doing what they are not
wanted to do, and that with
an affectation of innocence
that materially aggravates
their deliberate offense.

* * * * * * * * * *

**Helen Winslow,
American writer (1851–1938)**

You have now learned to see

That cats are much like you and me

— . — . — . — . —

T. S. Eliot, American-born
British poet (1888–1965)

I have studied many
philosophers and many cats.
The wisdom of cats is infinitely
Superior.

Hippolyte Taine, French critic,
historian (1828–1893)